STRAIGHT ARROW's

Manual of Indian Lore

BOOK 1

STRAIGHT ARROW's

Manual of Indian Lore

BOOK 1

GEORGE FRANGOULIS

The Farmstead Press

STRAIGHT ARROW's
Manual of Indian Lore
BOOK 1

Copyright 2014 by George Frangoulis.

All rights reserved. No part of this book may be transmitted or reproduced in any form by any means without permission in writing from the publisher.

Printed in the United States of America. First printing, 2014.

ISBN: 978-1-312-37942-8
George Frangoulis
715 Canyon Rd. N.
Tuscaloosa, AL 35406

ABOUT STRAIGHT ARROW AND "INJUN-UITY" MANUAL

By Roland Anderson

Straight Arrow was a fictional American Indian character. He was portrayed as a Comanche Indian orphan raised by whites as "Steve Adams" (same initials as "Straight Arrow"). Each Straight Arrow tale had Steve reverting to his true "secret Indian identity" in order to right some wrong, often committed against the Indians. In these efforts Steve was assisted by his golden palomino horse, Fury, and his grizzled side-kick, Packy McCloud.

Straight Arrow first made his first appearances almost simultaneously on a radio program and on "Injun-uity cards." These two projects were tightly coordinated projects backed by the National Biscuit Company and its advertising agency, McCann-Erickson. After a six month test-run on a local radio station in California, the radio series and the publication of the Injun-uity cards ran parallel with each other from 1949 to 1952.

In addition to the Injun-uity cards and the radio program, Straight Arrow appeared in a comic book and a newspaper comic strip. Publication of the comic book and the newspaper series were somewhat out of phase with the coordinated double-whammy mutual marketing support campaigns of the radio program and Injun-uity cards.

Both the comic book and the newspaper series started up about a year after the radio and Injun-uity card versions. But the newspaper series lasted only about a year, ending in late summer 1951. The comic book was more long-lasting, published from 1950 all the way up until 1956, a good five years longer than Straight Arrow's other incarnations.

Straight Arrow also gave rise to a great number of what at the time were called "novelties." Nabisco sold the rights to use its Straight Arrow figure on products like toys and clothing. While such things had previously occurred on a lesser scale, the enormity of the phenomenon in connection with Straight Arrow can surely rank it as an early example of modern merchandising.

STRAIGHT ARROW

"INJUN-UITY" Manual

STRAIGHT ARROW

INJUN-UITY INDEX

Page No.	Subject
1	COVER
2	INJUN-UITY INDEX
3	ROPE HOISTS
4	INDIAN TOOLS
5	INDIAN CAMP FIRES
6	INDIAN OVEN...COOLER
7	INDIAN GRILL or SPIT
8	INDIAN TEPEE
9	BRUSH SHELTER
10	PROPER CAMP
11	INDIAN LOOM
12	PAPOOSE CARRIAGE
13	INDIAN FOOT BRIDGE
14	INDIAN RAFT
15	INDIAN BOW MAKING
16	BOW STRINGING...CARE
17	ARROW MAKING
18	ARCHERY
19	POISONOUS SNAKES
20	DISTANCE SIGNALS
21	WATER SIGNALS
22	DANGER SIGNALS
23	HELP SIGNALS
24	ORIENTATION—Part 1
25	ORIENTATION—Part 2
26	TRACKING GAME (Veg.)
27	TRACKING GAME (Carn.)
28	POINTS OF A HORSE
29	INDIAN PONIES
30	ROPE HALTER or BRIDLE HORSEMANSHIP:
31	PROPER MOUNTING
32	PROPER POSTURE
33	HANDLING Your Mount
34	HELPING Your Mount
35	TRAVOIS or DRAG
36	ANIMAL TRICKS

When you put my Injun-uities into use, always respect the rights and property of others. Ask permission before selecting your campsite or using nature's materials belonging to others.

This Injun-uity Manual will help you be resourceful in the woods, in open country, at home, in school, in play, and at work.

"This manual was prepared by Fred L. Meagher, Indian illustrator and authority, for NABISCO SHREDDED WHEAT."

STRAIGHT ARROW

ROPE HOISTS

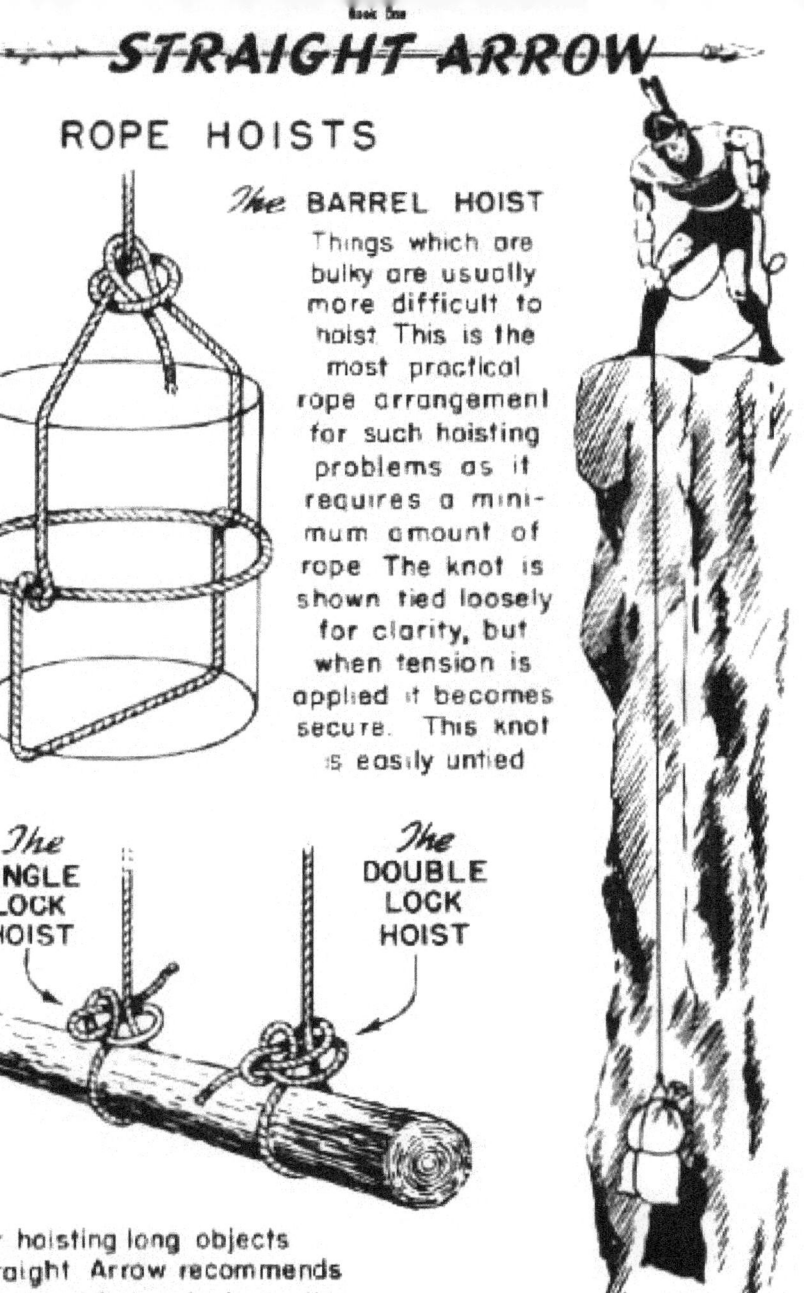

The BARREL HOIST

Things which are bulky are usually more difficult to hoist. This is the most practical rope arrangement for such hoisting problems as it requires a minimum amount of rope. The knot is shown tied loosely for clarity, but when tension is applied it becomes secure. This knot is easily untied.

The SINGLE LOCK HOIST

The DOUBLE LOCK HOIST

For hoisting long objects Straight Arrow recommends the use of the single or the double lock hoist.

If you have enough rope for only one hitch the lifting is made easier by hitching to the middle of the object.

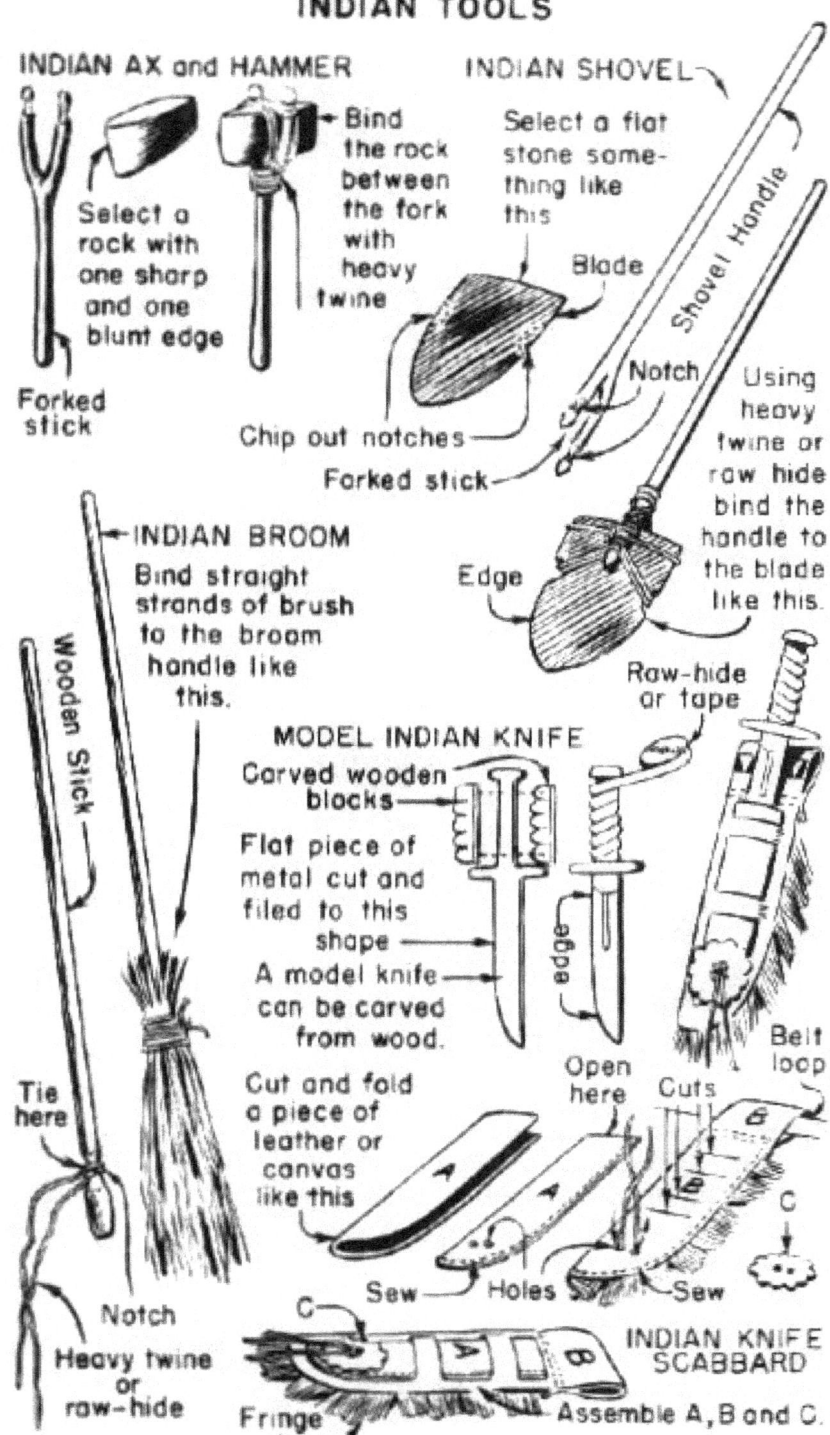

STRAIGHT ARROW

CAMP FIRES

An Indian sleep fire is made like this:

It is simple to keep it burning throughout the night by merely pushing the log spokes towards the center.

An Indian Roaster is made like this............

The heat is reflected by the logs and the smoke does not touch the roast........

"BASTING"...Place bowl here to catch juice for pouring over the roast.

See Page No. 7 for making the spit

An Indian Boiler is made like this

An Indian stove is made like this. Use dry stones and select a thin flat one for the stove top...

Straight Arrow says "Make sure you do not build fires where there is any danger of the fire spreading".

STRAIGHT ARROW

INDIAN OVEN :

Straight Arrow says to be sure to cover your oven with sand while it is baking to protect the feet of your dog, other animals or any small children that may be in camp.

INDIAN COOLER

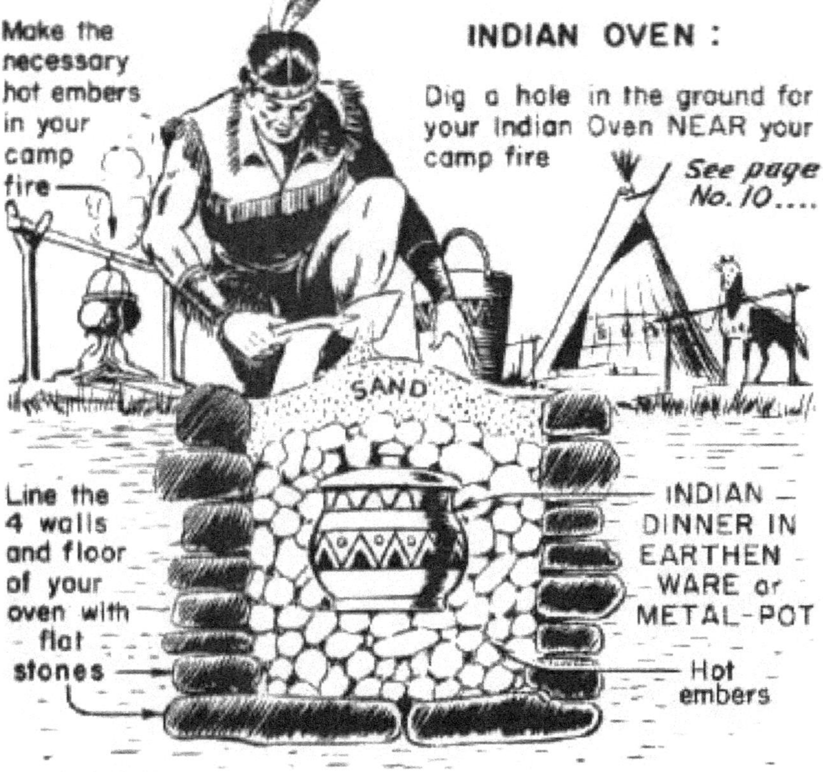

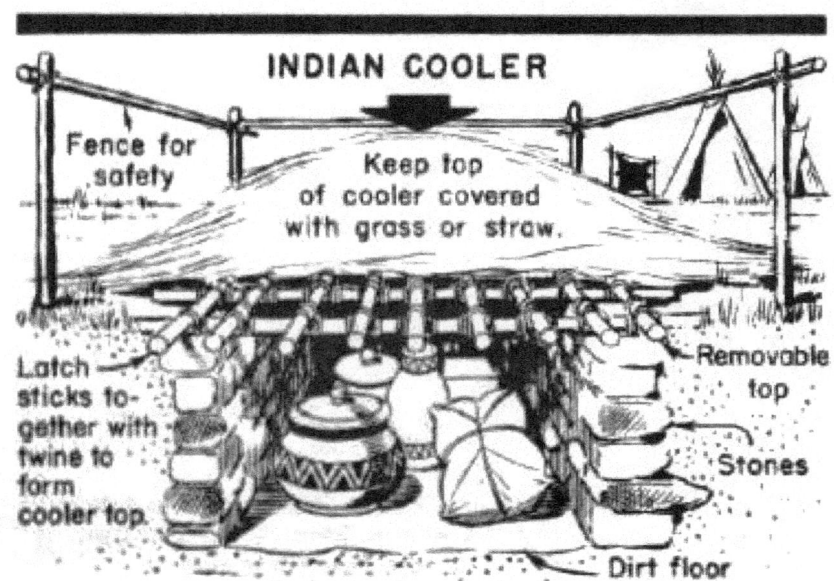

STRAIGHT ARROW

INDIAN GRILL or SPIT

Select a piece of green brush that is forked to form a shaft and crank. Cut off the excess branches so that you have something that looks like this.

Don't use dead brush.

Make 3 or 4 wooden pegs from green brush. Sharpen one end of each peg like a pencil.

Water-soak the part of the shaft which will be over the fire.

Wrap your fish, game or meat around the water soaked part of the shaft and fasten with the wooden pegs as shown.

Drive two forked, green brush stakes into the ground on each side of the fire like this—

Cradle the shaft in the forks as shown.

A wall of stones around your fire will help to drive the heat up from the coals.

Slowly turn the crank while you grill your fish or game over hot coals, (not over a smoking fire or high flames.)

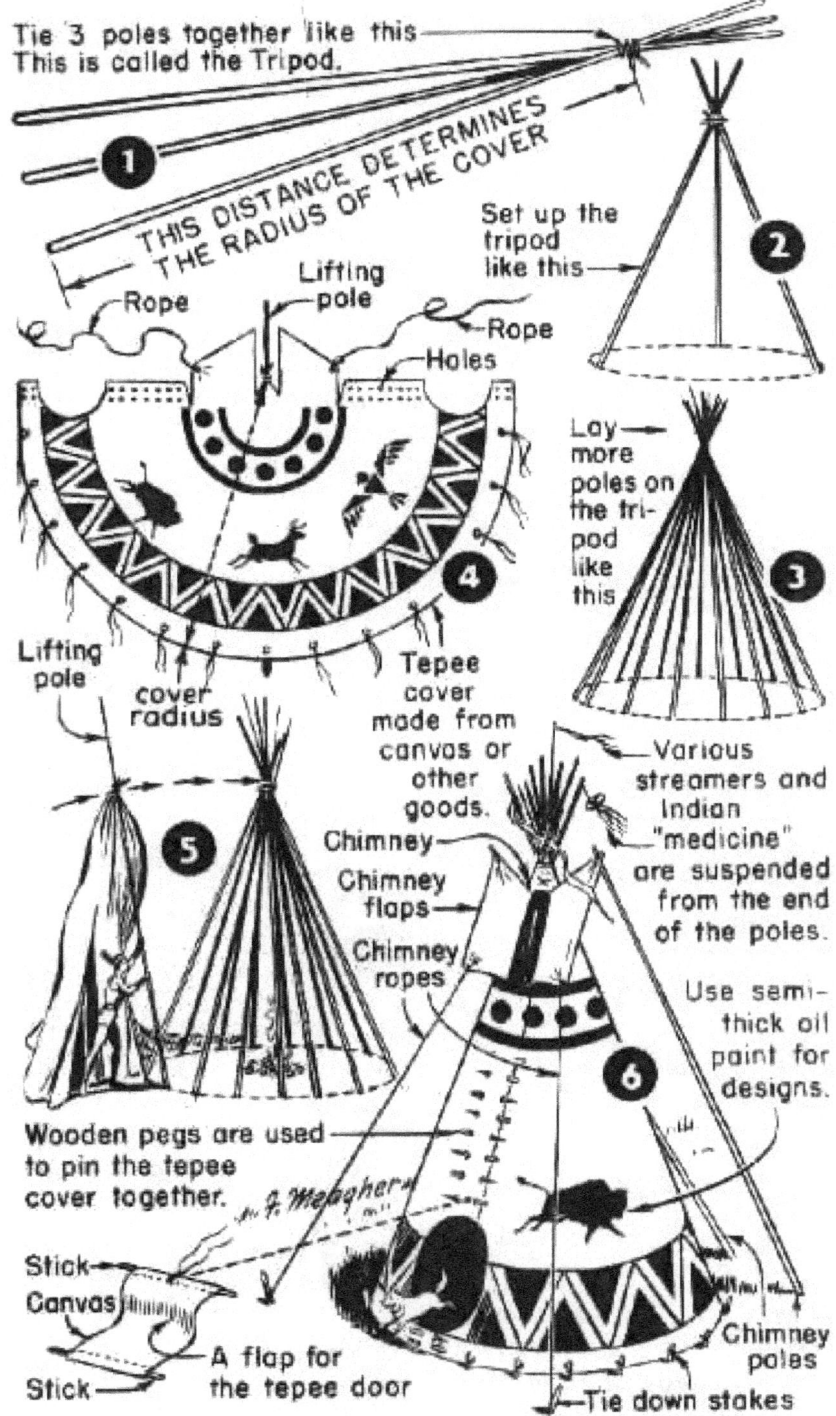

STRAIGHT ARROW

BRUSH SHELTER

The Foundation and main members of your shelter should be formed like this.

Main posts should be forked.

Basket-weave brush, spruce or pine bows, or even long grass through the stakes like this.

Drive these stakes in the ground

Use sapling poles to form the roof rafters and weave the brush, etc. through the poles in the same manner as used on the sides.

By building two shelters over the same main cross pole you can build a BRUSH HOUSE

Dig a trench around your shelter to keep out the rain water.

Straight Arrow suggests that you obtain permission before cutting down any sapling or brush.

STRAIGHT ARROW

INDIAN LOOM

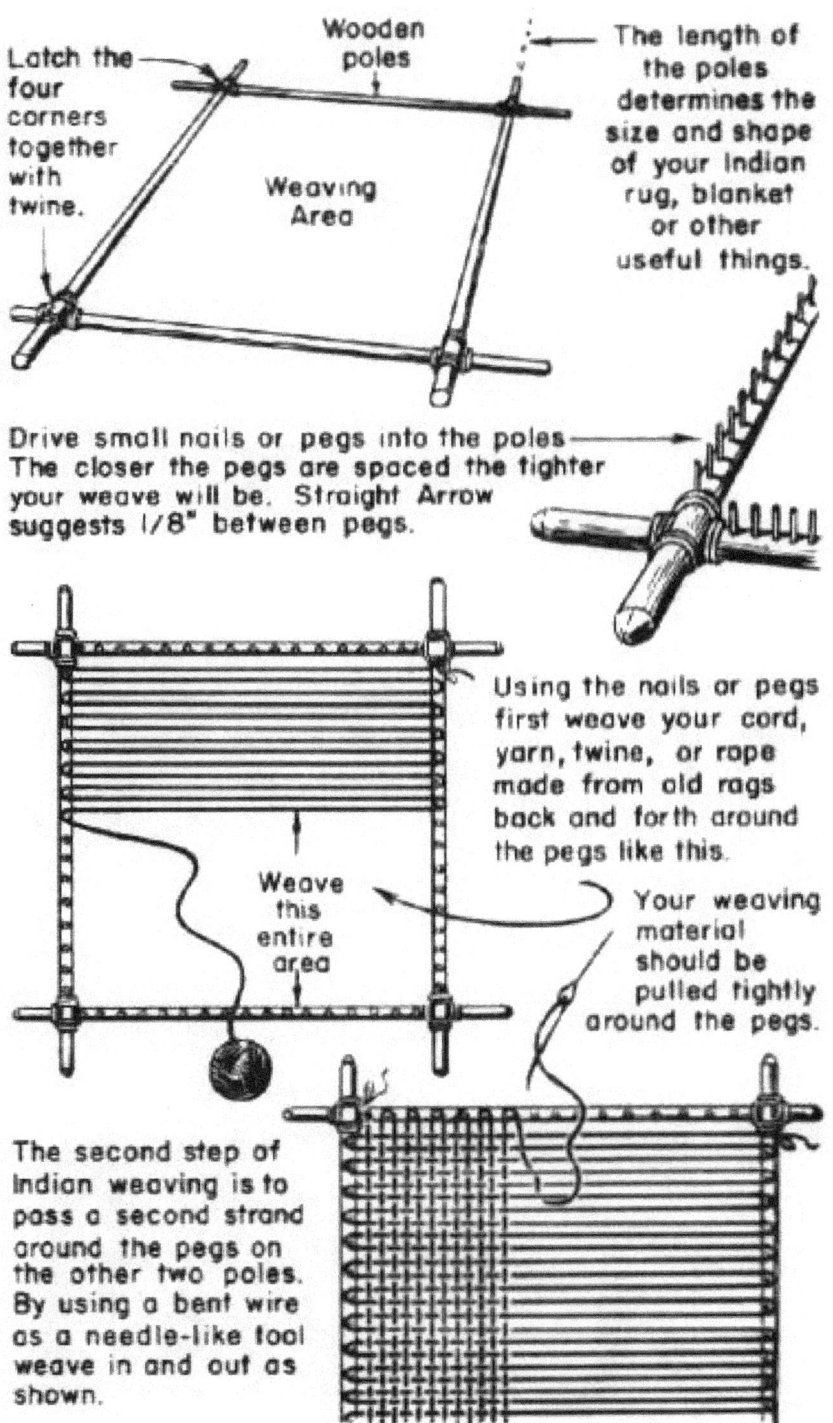

Latch the four corners together with twine.

Wooden poles

The length of the poles determines the size and shape of your Indian rug, blanket or other useful things.

Weaving Area

Drive small nails or pegs into the poles. The closer the pegs are spaced the tighter your weave will be. Straight Arrow suggests 1/8" between pegs.

Using the nails or pegs first weave your cord, yarn, twine, or rope made from old rags back and forth around the pegs like this.

Weave this entire area

Your weaving material should be pulled tightly around the pegs.

The second step of Indian weaving is to pass a second strand around the pegs on the other two poles. By using a bent wire as a needle-like tool weave in and out as shown.

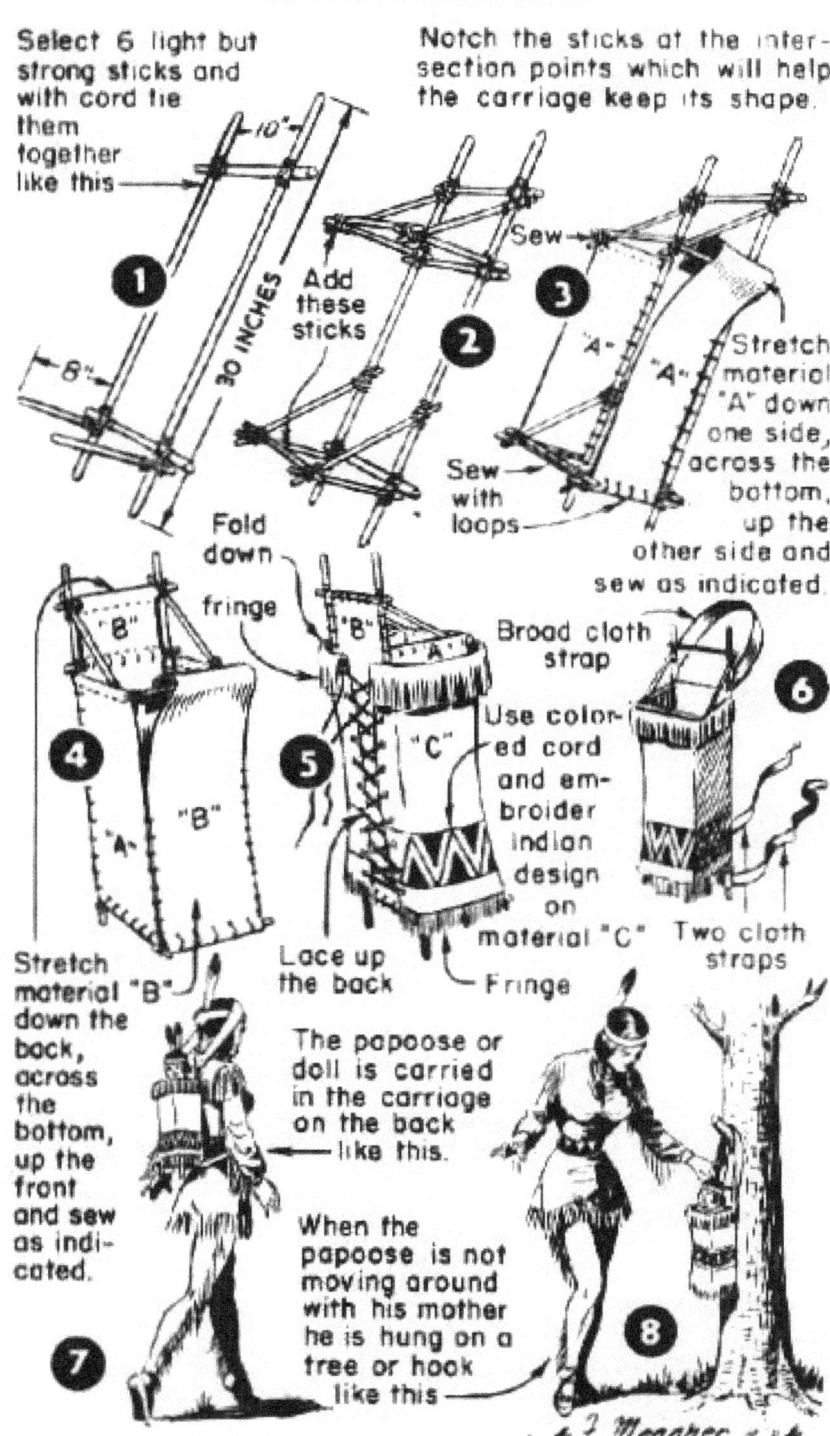

STRAIGHT ARROW

INDIAN FOOT BRIDGE

Anchor both ends of the log with rocks.

If possible select a tree near the bank of the stream. Cut it to fall across the stream as shown. If such a tree is not available float one down stream to the desired location.

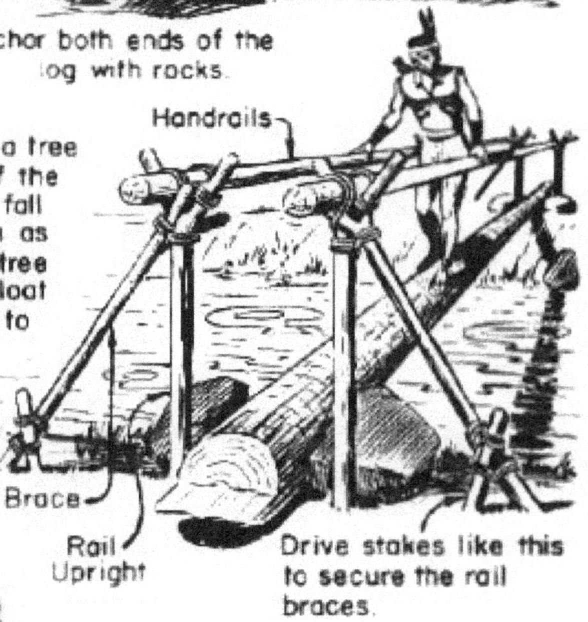

Handrails

Brace

Rail Upright

Drive stakes like this to secure the rail braces.

The handrail should be strong but not too heavy.

The rail uprights are forked and sunk one foot into the ground. Use forked sticks as braces and securely tie all connection points with rope or flexible roots.

— F. Meagher

STRAIGHT ARROW
INDIAN RAFT

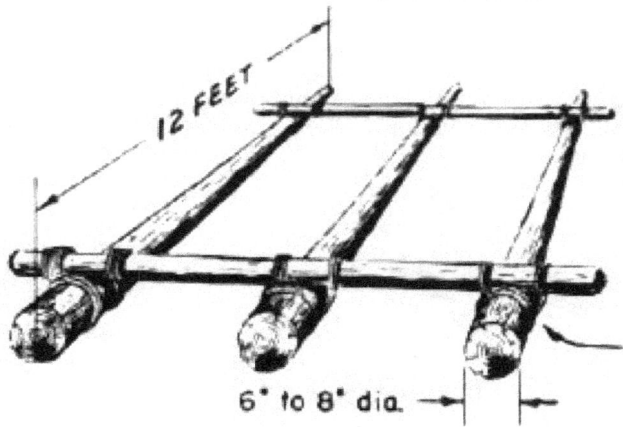

Select three logs 6" to 8" in diameter and two logs 4" to 6" in diameter.

Using rope, lash them together like this.

12 FEET

6" to 8" dia.

Select more 4" to 6" diameter logs and lash them to the three larger logs like this —

This raft will carry two people with fishing and hunting equipment...

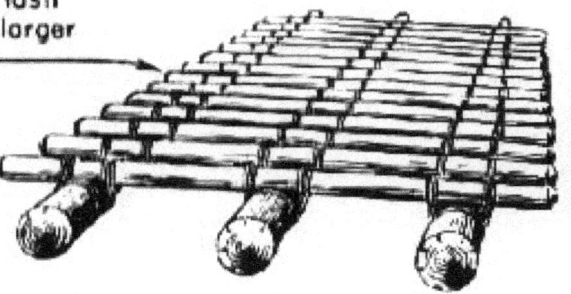

If the wind is in the right direction you can use a square rig sail like this -----

Mast
Rope loops

Lash the two cross poles to the mast with rope.

Lash the bottom of the mast in between 2 of the cross-logs.

J. Meagher

In addition to a sail.....
Straight Arrow propels his rafts in shallow water with a pole. In deep water he uses a paddle......

STRAIGHT ARROW

INDIAN BOW MAKING

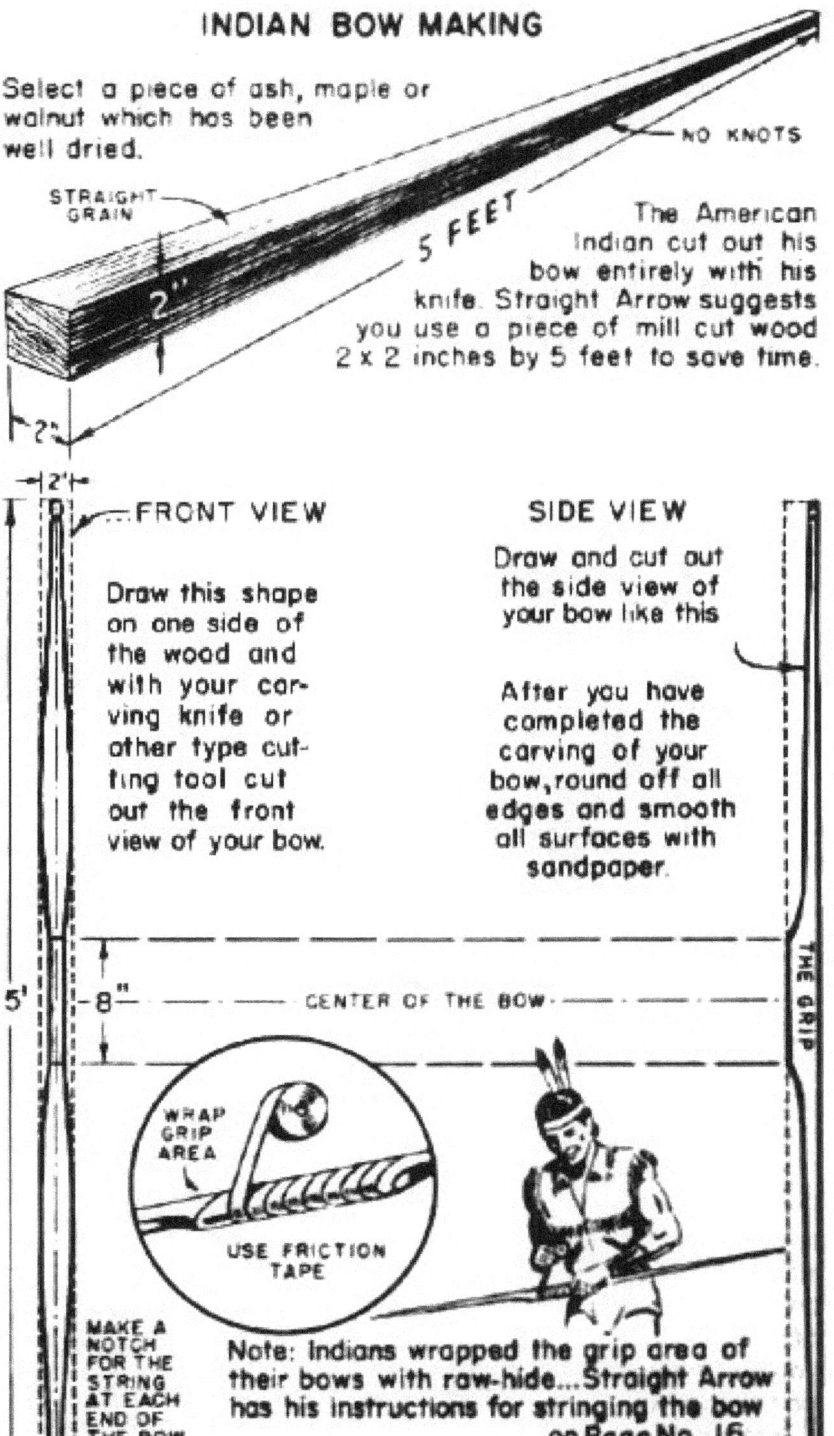

Select a piece of ash, maple or walnut which has been well dried.

STRAIGHT GRAIN

NO KNOTS

2"

5 FEET

The American Indian cut out his bow entirely with his knife. Straight Arrow suggests you use a piece of mill cut wood 2 x 2 inches by 5 feet to save time.

FRONT VIEW

Draw this shape on one side of the wood and with your carving knife or other type cutting tool cut out the front view of your bow.

SIDE VIEW

Draw and cut out the side view of your bow like this

After you have completed the carving of your bow, round off all edges and smooth all surfaces with sandpaper.

2"

5'

8"

CENTER OF THE BOW

THE GRIP

WRAP GRIP AREA

USE FRICTION TAPE

MAKE A NOTCH FOR THE STRING AT EACH END OF THE BOW

Note: Indians wrapped the grip area of their bows with raw-hide...Straight Arrow has his instructions for stringing the bow on Page No. 16

STRAIGHT ARROW

BOW STRINGING AND BOW CARE

When you have finished the shaping of your bow and have wrapped the grip area with tape, give the entire unit a coat of shellac.

Loop

Arrange your bow string like this using a raw hide string or good twine.

Tie firmly here

Leave a small loop here to be used for hanging up your bow

Stringing the bow

Straight Arrow holds this end of the bow with his left hand while at the same time he slips the loop into its notch.

Unstring your bow when it is not in use...

and

always hang it up by the small hang-up loop........

Note that this end of the bow is held against the side of the right foot.

TO CARRY ARROWS — Straight Arrow suggests that you make your own quiver out of leatherette, canvas, leather or any similar material.

Buckle
Strap should be adjustable
Strap
Sew sides
Sew one end of strap on here
Sew one end of strap on here.
Sew bottom

You can paint Indian designs on your quiver by using oil paint. (Use semi-thick paint.)

16

STRAIGHT ARROW
INDIAN ARROW MAKING

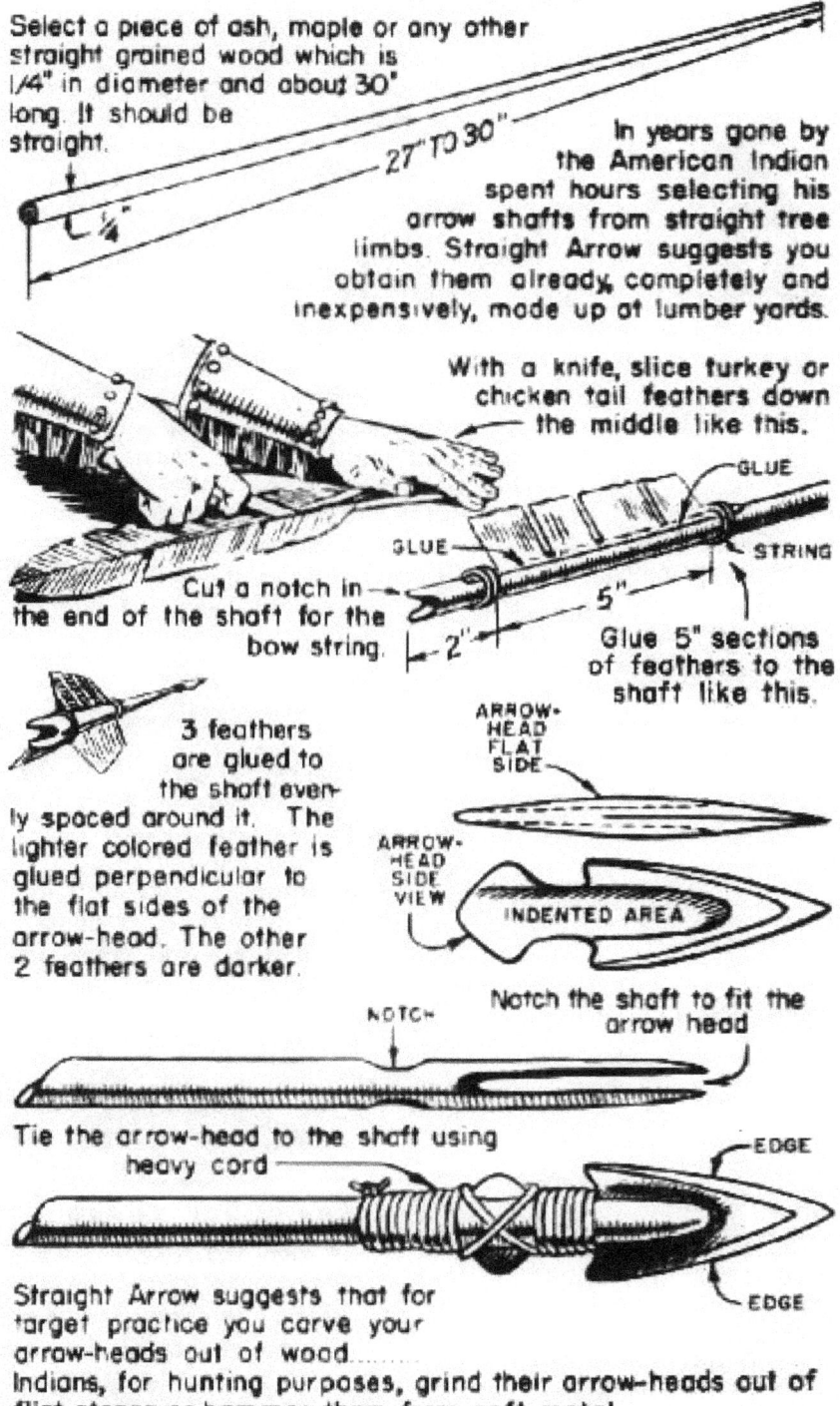

Select a piece of ash, maple or any other straight grained wood which is 1/4" in diameter and about 30" long. It should be straight.

In years gone by the American Indian spent hours selecting his arrow shafts from straight tree limbs. Straight Arrow suggests you obtain them already, completely and inexpensively, made up at lumber yards.

With a knife, slice turkey or chicken tail feathers down the middle like this.

Cut a notch in the end of the shaft for the bow string.

Glue 5" sections of feathers to the shaft like this.

3 feathers are glued to the shaft evenly spaced around it. The lighter colored feather is glued perpendicular to the flat sides of the arrow-head. The other 2 feathers are darker.

Notch the shaft to fit the arrow head

Tie the arrow-head to the shaft using heavy cord

Straight Arrow suggests that for target practice you carve your arrow-heads out of wood.
Indians, for hunting purposes, grind their arrow-heads out of flint stones or hammer them from soft metal.

STRAIGHT ARROW

POISONOUS SNAKE RECOGNITION

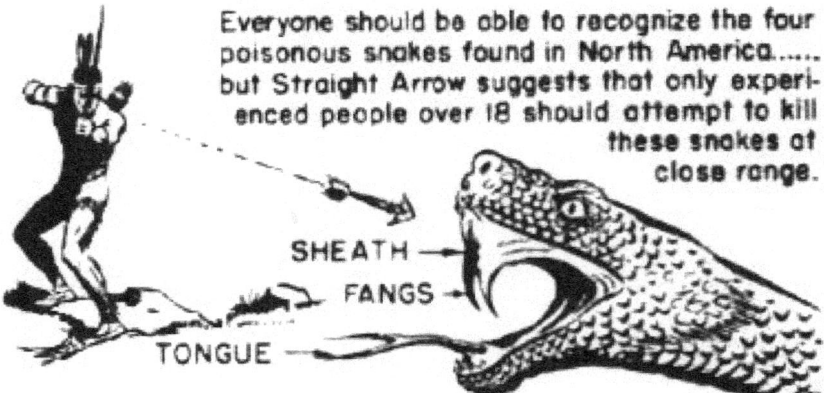

Everyone should be able to recognize the four poisonous snakes found in North America...... but Straight Arrow suggests that only experienced people over 18 should attempt to kill these snakes at close range.

SHEATH
FANGS
TONGUE

Note diamond shaped head

All poisonous snakes have a diamond shaped head when viewed from above. When their mouths are open large fangs are easily seen protruding from a large white area called the sheath.

The RATTLESNAKE...... is easily recognized by the rattles on the end of its tail.

The COPPERHEAD is reddish brown in color with the color the brightest on its head. Its back is marked with about fifteen "hour-glass" shaped marks of dark brown.

The WATER MOCCASIN.... has markings similar to the Copperhead but it is lighter in color. Opens its mouth very wide...has extra large fangs.

The CORAL SNAKE.... is rich red in color with black and yellow bands across its back..... It is found in the Southern U.S, Central and South America.

STRAIGHT ARROW

"ARCHERY"

1. Hold the center of bow with left hand. Insert arrow perpendicular to the string.

2. Arrow is held lightly between first 2 fingers. Arrow lays on the bow. Arrow fork straddles string.

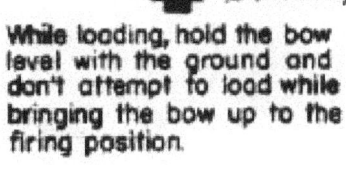

While loading, hold the bow level with the ground and don't attempt to load while bringing the bow up to the firing position.

3. The odd colored feather should be up.

The left side of the body should face the target.

The arrow is not sighted but is aimed as you would when throwing a baseball.

4. Forearm in line with arrow.

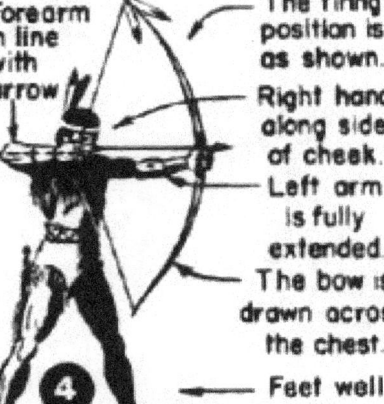

The firing position is as shown.
- Right hand along side of cheek.
- Left arm is fully extended.
- The bow is drawn across the chest.
- Feet well apart.

5. Each foot should line up with the target like this — practice, strong nerves and good judgment make the marksman.

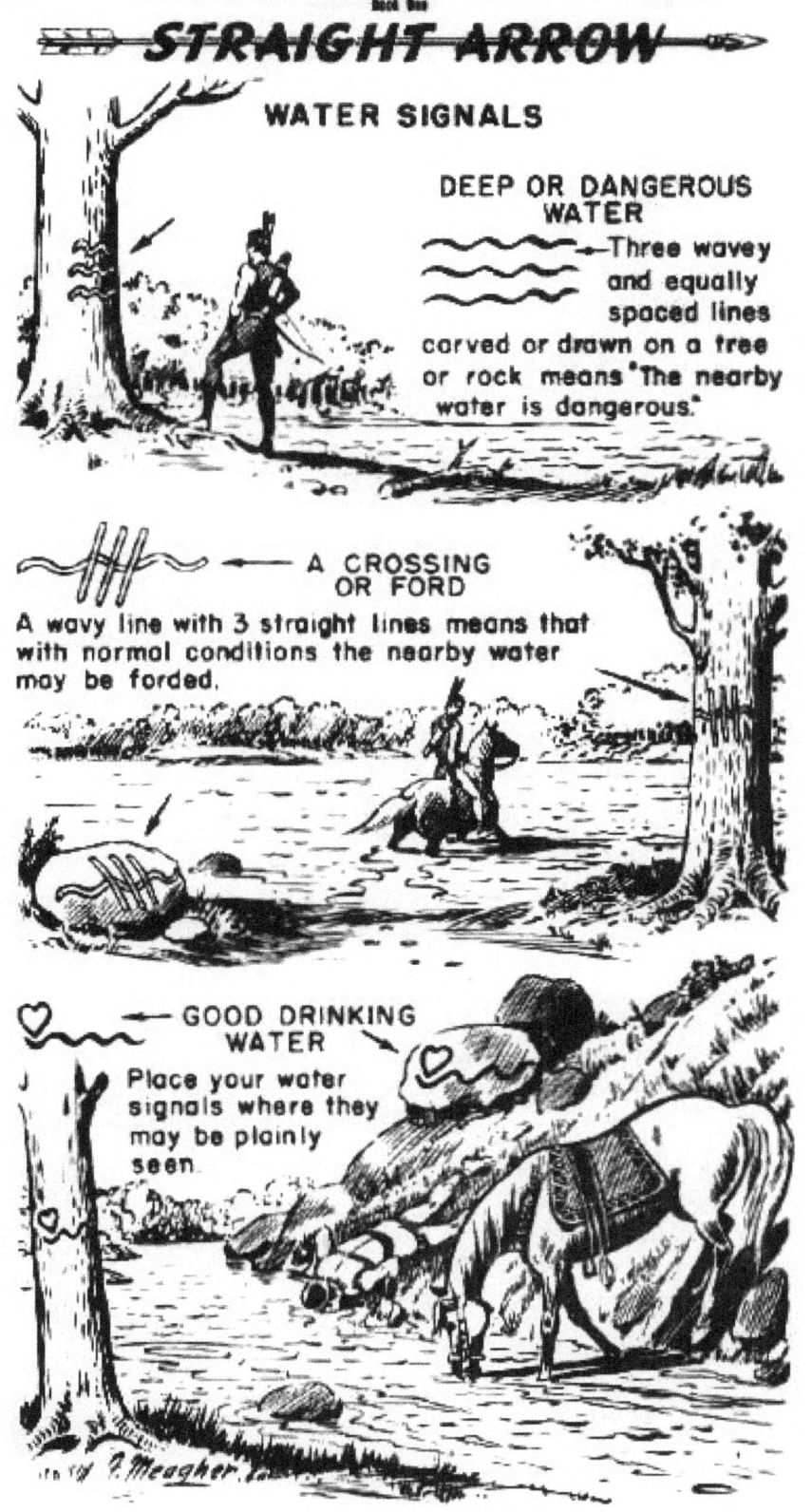

STRAIGHT ARROW

DANGER SIGNALS

These Indian Danger Signals are still used today... Straight Arrow wants you to learn to use and recognize them... you may someday save a life.

A bundle of 3 sticks hanging from a cross-bar, tree or post means:..."Quicksand or deep mud nearby". A permanent arrow should be cut into a nearby tree or stump to indicate the direction of the danger.

One stick hanging from a crossbar, tree or post means..."Deep holes or possible cave-ins are nearby". Straight Arrow uses the cross-bar, or a series of cross-bars, to warn people and animals after dark.

Two cross-bars with a stone suspended from the top bar means:... "All nearby water is bad drinking water.... or even poisonous"............
This diagram drawn on the ground means the same thing..... but Straight Arrow says: "Use the cross-bars as they will not wash or wear away."

"Dangerous animals nearby."

"Cliff or drop-off ahead" ...also used as a warning to fast riding horsemen to slow down because there is dangerous footing ahead.

STRAIGHT ARROW

HELP SIGNALS

The original INDIAN HELP SIGNALS shown here have saved many lives in rough country in the past, and they will save many more in the future. Today they are used by many outdoorsmen as well as Indians.

These 3 signals mean "NEED HELP... THIS WAY!"

3 equally spaced stakes with an arrow drawn on the ground to indicate your direction.

3 equally spaced bundles of grass with an arrow drawn on the ground.

3 equally spaced piles of rocks (3 rocks each pile) with an arrow drawn on the ground.

If you are hurt or lost and have a gun, 3 shots in quick succession mean "HELP".

3 bark-like yells in succession also mean "HELP".

3 smoke columns from 3 equally spaced fires mean "HELP".

STRAIGHT ARROW

ORIENTATION—Part I

Some reasons why Indians never get lost.

While traveling through darkness or through strange wooded areas an Indian will constantly break off twigs so that, if necessary, he can follow his own trail back. Occasionally he will cut chips from the trees...

When traveling in strange stony areas it is natural for him to pile 3 or 4 stones, one on top of another, or form arrows with small stones, to mark his trail.⟶

It is not unusual to see an Indian mark his trail by placing a forked stick like this.... or to cut a stick to form an arrow and lay it on the ground.

In grassy areas he will continually tie clumps of grass together using strands of grass as cord...

...in barren or desert areas he will mark his trail with arrows drawn on the ground.

Straight Arrow says you can have fun playing games using STRAIGHT ARROW ORIENTATION.

STRAIGHT ARROW

ORIENTATION - Part 2

Some reasons why Indians never get lost.

It is in an Indians blood to be aware of danger from the rear; therefore, he constantly looks back. He also observes the landmarks to his rear which makes it easy for him to return. A white man usually fails to do this and therefore often gets lost.

When traveling in a strange area where water is scarce an Indian will pick up the trail of a grazing animal and follow it to drinking water. Grazing animals drink often and know where the water is in the area in which they are grazing...

If an Indian does lose his bearings he will naturally travel a valley until he comes upon a stream.... He will always travel DOWN STREAM because it will take him to people and information... Straight Arrow suggests that you learn his ORIENTATION ...it may someday save you from exposure or even save your LIFE.

STRAIGHT ARROW

TRACKING - VEGETARIAN ANIMALS
(Plant eating animls)

A DEER, traveling at a slow lope or canter (a sheep or goat will make a similar but wider foot print).

Deer tracks on firm soil.

Appearance of deer tracks in mud or snow.

— RABBIT TRACKS —

A BARE-FOOTED HORSE

....A horse with shoes on......

CATTLE, BUFFALO or MOOSE....

Traveling at a walk......

In forests, near towns and farms, dog, cat and rat tracks are often confused with wild game. Straight Arrow suggests you learn dog, cat, and rat tracks before attempting to track other animals or game.

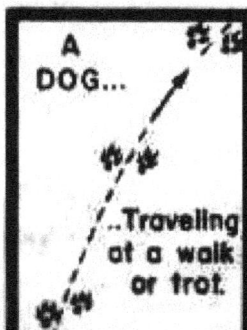

A DOG... ..Traveling at a walk or trot.

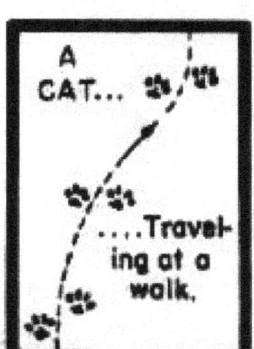

A CAT... ....Traveling at a walk.

A RAT... Traveling at a trot.

STRAIGHT ARROW

TRACKING CARNIVOROUS (Meat eating game)

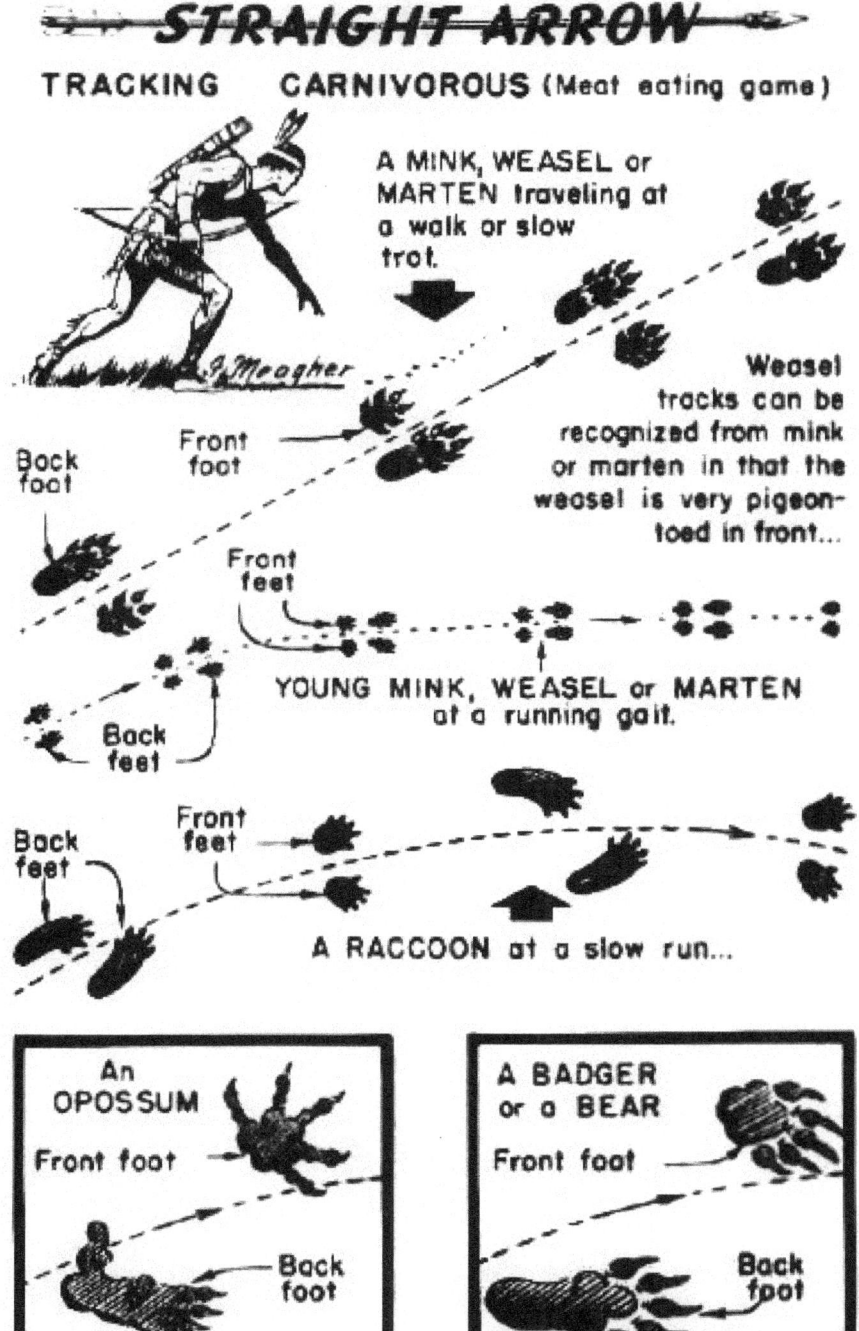

A MINK, WEASEL or MARTEN traveling at a walk or slow trot.

Weasel tracks can be recognized from mink or marten in that the weasel is very pigeon-toed in front...

YOUNG MINK, WEASEL or MARTEN at a running gait.

A RACCOON at a slow run...

An OPOSSUM Front foot — Back foot

A BADGER or a BEAR Front foot — Back foot

Carnivorous game, while hunting, usually travels a zig-zag course but if they think they are being followed they take a rather straight course. Straight Arrow recommends tracking practice in your nearby fields and woods and you will soon become an expert.

STRAIGHT ARROW

POINTS OF A HORSE

Cattle, Sheep, Deer, or any other grazing animal.

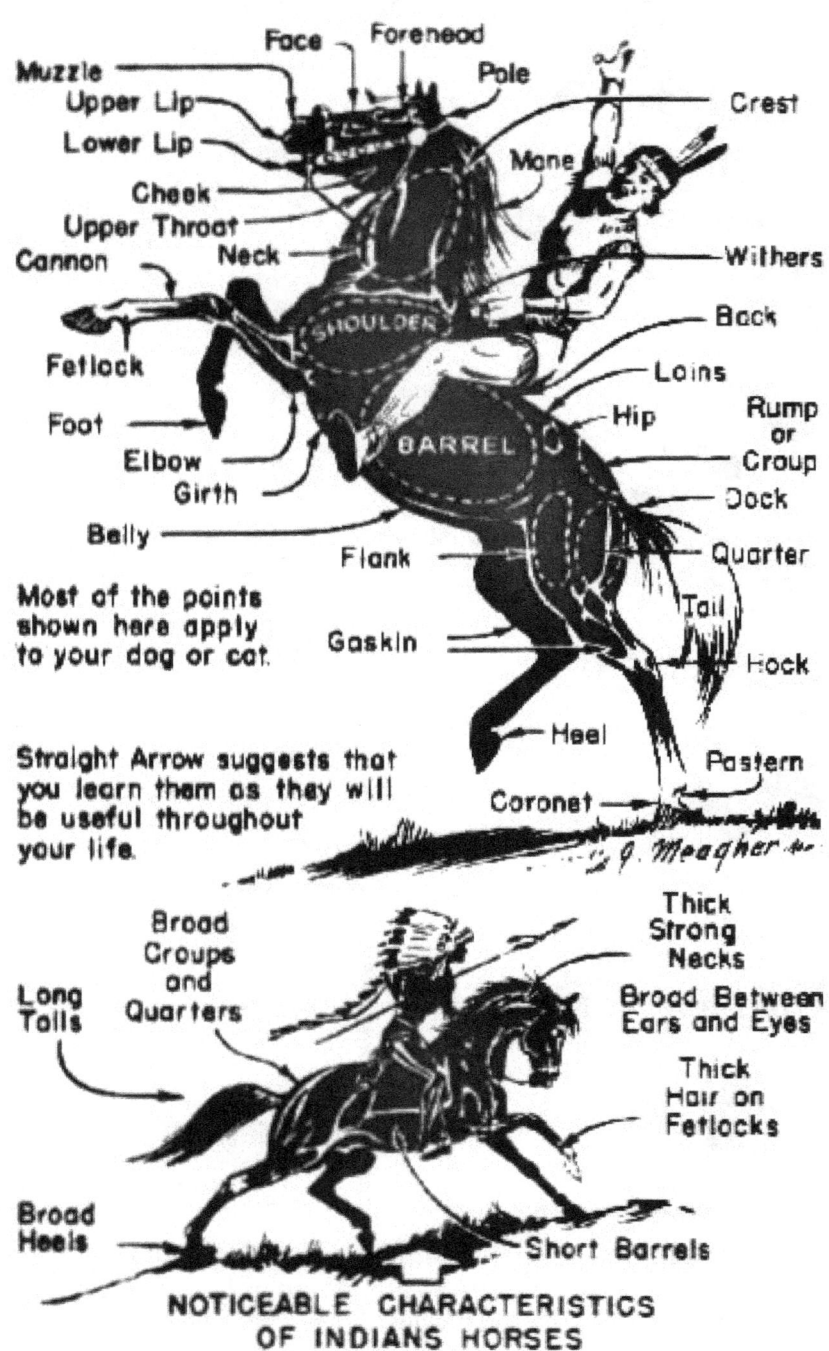

Most of the points shown here apply to your dog or cat.

Straight Arrow suggests that you learn them as they will be useful throughout your life.

NOTICEABLE CHARACTERISTICS OF INDIANS HORSES

STRAIGHT ARROW
INDIAN HORSE RECOGNITION

The PALOMINO BEING GOLD OF COLOR IS THE MOST DISTINGUISHED OF INDIAN HORSES. TO BE GENUINE IT MUST BE GOLD ...IT MUST HAVE A WHITE TAIL AND MANE. IT MAY HAVE WHITE SOCKS BUT NO WHITE SPOTS ABOVE THE KNEES, EXCEPT, IT MAY HAVE A WHITE STAR, STRIPE OR BLAZE ON ITS FACE..

The APPALOOSA MUST HAVE BLACK & WHITE.....OR BROWN AND WHITE FRECKLE-LIKE SPOTS ON A WHITE COAT. TO BE GENUINE IT MUST HAVE THIS COLORING ON ITS RUMP.

The PIEBALD MUST BE COLORED IN BLACK AND WHITE SPOTS.

The PINTO... MUST BE COLORED IN BROWN AND WHITE SPOTS.

The PAINT... MUST BE COLORED IN BLACK, BROWN, WHITE AND ANY OTHER COLOR.

Although several other horse colors appear among Indian horses......those shown here are known throughout the world as American Indian. Indian horses are tough and most always have sound legs and feet

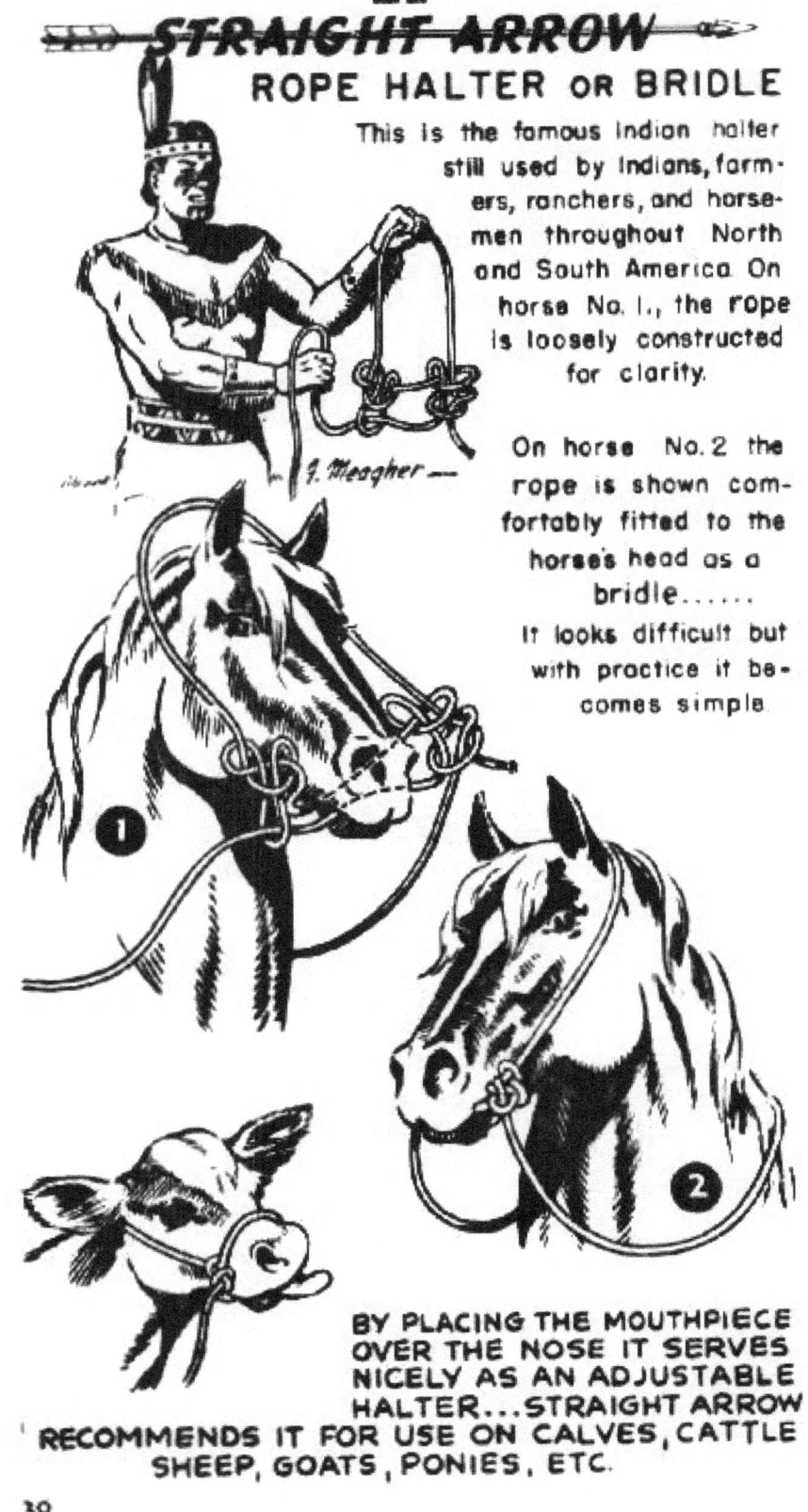

STRAIGHT ARROW
ROPE HALTER OR BRIDLE

This is the famous Indian halter still used by Indians, farmers, ranchers, and horsemen throughout North and South America. On horse No. 1, the rope is loosely constructed for clarity.

On horse No. 2 the rope is shown comfortably fitted to the horse's head as a bridle......
It looks difficult but with practice it becomes simple.

BY PLACING THE MOUTHPIECE OVER THE NOSE IT SERVES NICELY AS AN ADJUSTABLE HALTER...STRAIGHT ARROW RECOMMENDS IT FOR USE ON CALVES, CATTLE SHEEP, GOATS, PONIES, ETC.

STRAIGHT ARROW
HORSEMANSHIP - PROPER MOUNTING

1. Always mount your steed from his left side.* Gather up the reins in your left hand. Pull his head a trifle towards you with the left rein.

2. Stand along side your steed's left shoulder and face his rear. Place your left foot in the left stirrup like this.

*Some Indians mount from the right

4. Swing up to this position and always stop here long enough to touch or click your heels. This provides you with good form and balance.

3. If your steed should start to walk or run away...by having his head pulled towards you he is forced to immediately circle which makes it simple for you to stop him.

4. Still holding the reins in your left hand swing your right leg over his rump. At this step you may release the pull on the left rein.

5. Settle yourself on his back and find the right stirrup with your right toe. Your knees should be slightly bent with your feet in the stirrups.

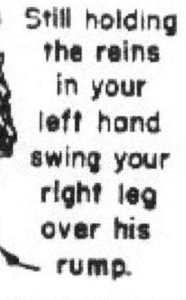

31

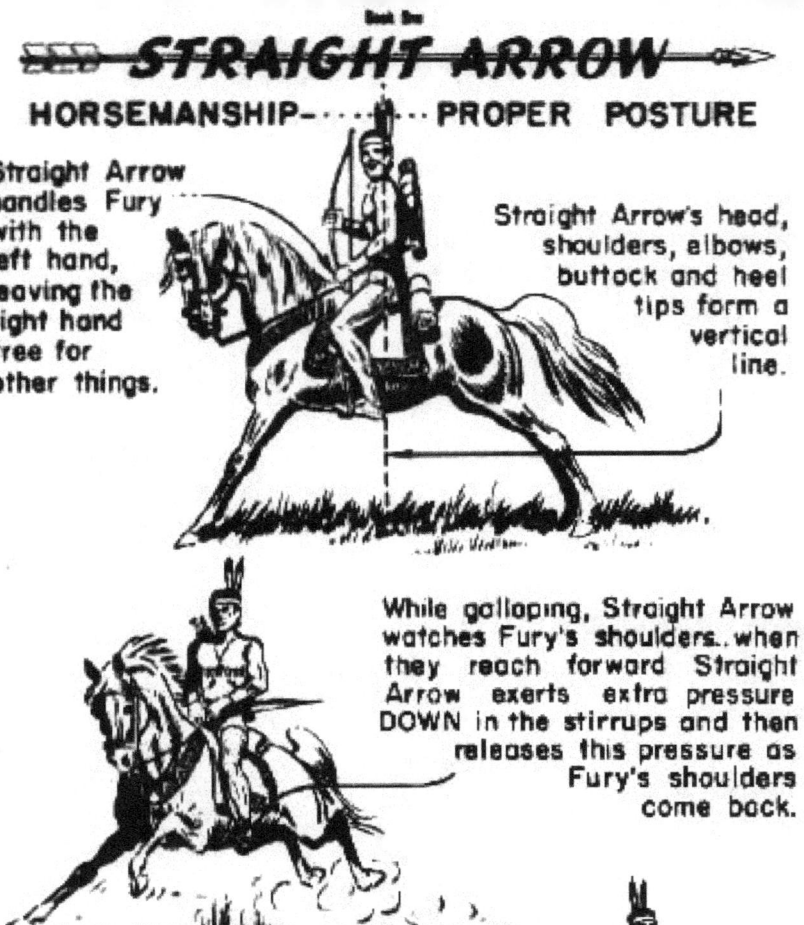

STRAIGHT ARROW

HORSEMANSHIP- HANDLING YOUR MOUNT

To start from a standing position Straight Arrow leans foreward.... at the same time running the reins up along Fury's neck and tapping him with his heels. This is a motion to urge him forward which any riding horse will understand. After Fury starts, Straight Arrow takes up the slack in the reins but does not pull on Fury's mouth.

Most riding horses are "bridle-wise" which means they respond to the pressure of the reins across the back of their necks. To turn Fury, Straight Arrow moves his left hand to the left for a left turn and to the right for a right turn.

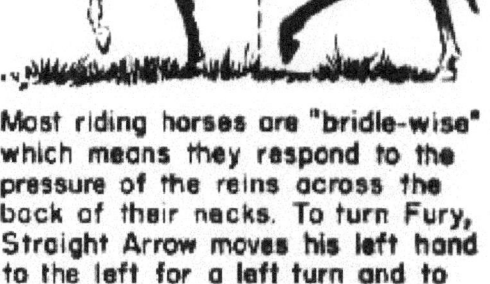

To put Fury into a gallop, Straight Arrow briskly brushes Fury's sides with his legs and at the same time flaps the reins in a forward motion on Fury's neck.

When going down grade, Straight Arrow gives Fury his head (that is slack in the reins)...and leans forward (not back)....... this helps Fury obtain better footing. To stop Fury, Straight Arrow pulls on the reins and leans back.

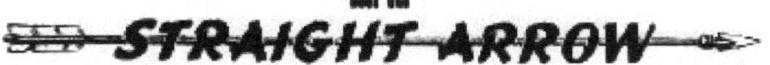

HORSEMANSHIP- HELPING YOUR MOUNT

Straight Arrow carries his elbows comfortably close to his sides and he does not allow them to flap out in the air which is considered very bad form and balance.

His knees are slightly flexed when his feet are comfortably in the stirrups with his heels down.

Straight Arrow encourages Fury to carry his head just right which makes smoother riding............

...JUST RIGHT

When a horse carries his head just right he will hold his tail right, pick up his feet and take pride in himself.

WRONG... too high

WRONG... too low

By talking to Fury and with slight pressure on the reins Straight Arrow soon taught Fury the proper place to carry his head.

Notice that Straight Arrow keeps his hands low near Fury's withers. This helps Fury's carriage, and he will not stumble.

STRAIGHT ARROW

ANIMAL TRICKS

How to teach your Pal to Kneel and Pray

Straight Arrow taught Fury to bow, first tying a rope to Fury's halter, then passing it between his front legs, up his right shoulder and across his withers, (See page No 28) Straight Arrow then pulled on the rope which exerted downward pressure on Fury's withers and at the same time brought his head down.

By bending Fury's left leg with his left hand while continuing the pull on the rope and repeating the word "KNEEL" Fury knelt ⟶

"PRAY"

He then rewarded Fury with words, pats and a carrot. He repeated this practice many times at frequent intervals until Fury would kneel without the pull of the rope. "KNEEL"

From the kneeling position Straight Arrow taught Fury to pray by continuing the pull on the rope and repeating the word "PRAY".
A rope is used to help put a horse in position until he learns what his master wants him to do.

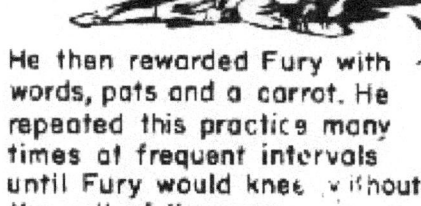

Squeeze and push down on the withers

Push head down

Fold front legs under

Straight Arrow helped Fury to bow without the aid of the rope by touching him on the withers and knees with a whip.

— J. Meagher

Straight Arrow taught his dog to bow and pray using the same commands, but exerting pressure with his hands instead of the rope. You can teach your horse or dog tricks such as lying down, sitting-up, etc., in much the same manner